THROW AWAY KIDS

TOM SPENCE

THROW AWAY KIDS

Are we
concerned
enough to get
involved?

TATE PUBLISHING
AND ENTERPRISES, LLC

Throw Away Kids
Copyright © 2015 by Tom Spence. All rights reserved.

No part of this publication may be reproduced, stored in a retrieval system or transmitted in any way by any means, electronic, mechanical, photocopy, recording or otherwise without the prior permission of the author except as provided by USA copyright law.

Scripture quotations marked (MSG) are taken from *The Message.* Copyright © 1993, 1994, 1995, 1996, 2000, 2001, 2002. Used by permission of NavPress Publishing Group.

Scripture quotations marked (NIV) are taken from the *Holy Bible, New International Version*®, NIV®. Copyright © 1973, 1978, 1984 by Biblica, Inc.™ Used by permission of Zondervan. All rights reserved worldwide. www.zondervan.com

This book is designed to provide accurate and authoritative information with regard to the subject matter covered. This information is given with the understanding that neither the author nor Tate Publishing, LLC is engaged in rendering legal, professional advice. Since the details of your situation are fact dependent, you should additionally seek the services of a competent professional.

The opinions expressed by the author are not necessarily those of Tate Publishing, LLC.

Published by Tate Publishing & Enterprises, LLC
127 E. Trade Center Terrace | Mustang, Oklahoma 73064 USA
1.888.361.9473 | www.tatepublishing.com

Tate Publishing is committed to excellence in the publishing industry. The company reflects the philosophy established by the founders, based on Psalm 68:11,
"The Lord gave the word and great was the company of those who published it."

Book design copyright © 2015 by Tate Publishing, LLC. All rights reserved.
Cover design by Nino Carlo Suico
Interior design by Jomar Ouano

Published in the United States of America

ISBN: 978-1-68118-257-5
Family & Relationships / Parenting / General
15.03.06

God told them, "I've never quit loving you and never will.
Expect love, love, and more love!"

—Jeremiah 31:3 (*The Message*)

This short exposé is dedicated to those who love the children who are not loved by the parents.

It is a tribute to those who never seem to run out of love for the unloved.

It is a warning that if we become callous instead of courageous and don't start leading the parents who have given up, this cycle will repeat itself.

This is dedicated to the men and women of courage that have answered the calling which we know as parent.

This book commends those who instead of reacting with righteous anger toward the parents of these *throwaway kids*, chose instead to respond with the leadership of love.

Uncommon

Uncommon valor was a common virtue.

—Admiral Chester Nimitz

Upon witnessing the ubiquitous acts of courage and selfless compassion among Marines who fought in the Pacific in World War II, especially Iwo Jima, Admiral Nimitz spoke these five words: **"Uncommon valor was a common virtue."** They are cast upon the base of the Marine Memorial that overlooks our nation's capital and the graves of so many who died preserving our way of life.

The same such courage is needed among parents. It is needed on the home front. Such unique leadership must become common in this fight to save a lost generation and a valued way of life some may never come to know were we to lose this battle.

Forward

Does this happen where you live?
Children dropped off at school.
Children dropped off at day care.
Children dropped off at church.
Children who make their own meals.
Children with no set time to be home.
We are not talking about high school juniors and seniors.

This is the life of many children from the time they can walk and dress themselves until they move out of the house. Dare we call this environment a home?

TOM SPENCE

So many children in this country seem to be inconveniences to their parents.

So many children in this country have been regarded as property.

We are appalled when this is the culture of a distant country.

We can't believe that it was this way in ancient times.

We ignore it in our own backyard.

Many have mercy on the children of these parents—as we should.

Many do not speak the truth to the parents of these children.

What is that truth?

That many have abandoned parenting.

That many have forsaken the duties that go with the wonderful gift from God that we call children.

That we who know better have done nothing about addressing the root of the problem.

That together—those who know what's wrong and do nothing in collusion with those who don't seem to care about their children's welfare—we have created a generation of **Throwaway Kids**.

Are we content to just stand by and do nothing?

Do we have the courage to speak the truth in love to the parents?

Will we assist these parents who have abandoned their parental leadership role in becoming real parents?

Do we have the courage to confront without condemning?

Are we content with a generation of **Throwaway Kids**?

Don't pick on people, jump on their failures, criticize their faults—unless, of course, you want the same treatment. That critical spirit has a way of boomeranging. It's easy to see a smudge on your neighbor's face and be oblivious to the ugly sneer on your own. Do you have the nerve to say, "Let me wash your face for you," when your own face is distorted by contempt? It's this whole traveling road show mentality all over again, playing a holier-than-thou part instead of just living your part. Wipe that ugly sneer off your own face, and you might be fit to offer a washcloth to your neighbor.

—Matthew 7:1–5 (The Message)

TOM SPENCE

Just who are you to talk about someone else's kids?

That is a very fair question.

I don't like people or organizations or the government messing around with the inner workings of my family.

> We should be able to protect the domain that we call home and family.
> I don't like meddling in other people's business.
> So just who am I to talk about someone else's kids.
> I am the guy who sees the kids in dirty clothes.
> They are the same clothes the kid wore for the past two days.
> They smell like cigarette smoke.

> I am the guy who sees the kid with holes in his shoes and jeans.
> These are not designer holes for which you pay $40 extra.
> These are the holes that say, this is all I have.
> I am the guy who sees hungry kids every week.
> They eat the church meal as if they haven't eaten all week.
> That is sometimes the truth.

> I am the guy who sees the car almost come to a stop in the church parking lot.
> It won't come into the drivethrough awning.
> Someone might meet the car and talk to the driver.
> The kids get out and run to the church.
> They know we will love them here.

They run toward that love.
The car speeds away.

I am the guy who talks to the parent who asks if the church van can pick up his kids for VBS.

I tell him that he will have to come the first day to register them.
He says that he will just drive then.
During registration, he says that he can understand bringing his kids the first day.
But he shouldn't be bothered with it for the rest of the week.
He has no job and no other commitments.

I am the guy who gives kids in a school class a buck each.
The book fair is in town.
The parents sent no money.
I saw some of the parents buying beer and cigarettes the night before.
Sometimes the parents wait until I'm not around to buy these things.

I don't preach against alcohol or tobacco.
God made all things good.
Jesus made the best wine ever in AD thirty-something.
I would love to have a bottle of that.
I think they drank it all at the wedding in Cana.
I don't know of anyone who ended up with cancer from an occasional cigar.

TOM SPENCE

I have confronted parents when the church paid a past due water bill for $80.

The night before these same adults were buying cokes, chips, dip, cigarettes, and other junk food at the convenience store and at the convenience store price.

Many are offended when I tell them that the church is really paying for cigarettes and self gratification.

Parents run out of my office faster at the mention of the word *budget* than when I share the gospel of Jesus Christ.

Some will say, "That guy is just picking on smokers."

That's partially true.

If an adult chooses between his child's welfare and his personal addiction, yes, I will confront them.

I am that guy.

If an adult chooses between convenience store lunches every day and his kids go without, I will introduce him or her to the term *brown bag*.

I am that guy.

I have no problems with folks who spend their money on alcohol, tobacco, and even firearms.

There is a problem when it is done at the expense of necessities for the kids.

I am the guy who will say with as much love in my heart as I can muster when my human nature pleads with me to take some of these yahoos out back and beat some parenting skills into them, "Don't you think there is a better way to live."

God wants us to have good things.
He doesn't want us to spend our lives gratifying ourselves.

He tells us that if we seek his kingdom and his righteousness first, then he will provide the things that the greedy world lives for.

Too many parents have refused this counsel.
They say they believe in God.
Their words say, "I believe."
Their actions spit in God's face.
God will not be mocked.

The fruit of this self-centered lifestyle is a generation of *throwaway kids*.
Too many parents consider their children burdens instead of blessings.
They can't wait to get them into Head Start or public school.
It's free day care.

I am the guy who, growing up, had a good deal of freedom to play in my neighborhood.

TOM SPENCE

I am the guy who today sees very young children on the other side of town and their parents don't have a clue where they are or what they are doing. Neighborhoods are not what they used to be.

I am the guy who knows that on Wednesday night, about a third of the children who come for the church meal did not tell their parents where they were going.

> They did not tell them they were leaving the house.
> They did not tell them when they would be home.
> And the parents don't care.
> Sometimes the parents are high and don't care.
> Sometimes they just don't care.

> I am the guy who listens to the wife who can't pay her electric bill.
> Her husband lost his job.
> He won't come to the church.
> Sometimes he will come but not get out of the car.
> The bill hasn't been paid for three months.
> The husband just got a new truck two months ago.
> The monthly payments resemble a mortgage on a nice home.
> The family is on food stamps.
> The kids go without except for what we give them.
> I must say that it is a fine looking truck.

> The kids don't have three dollars for the field trip.
> It is a really fun trip.
> The school pays half.
> The parents have refused help with their budget for the past three years.

THROW AWAY KIDS

I am the guy who is in the middle of these pitiful episodes every week.

Perhaps ignorance is bliss.

If I did not know where so much of the money went or didn't see dirty, hungry kids, then I might not have a passion to speak the truth to parents.

Speaking the truth in love, we must call upon parents to cowboy up to their responsibilities.

Parents need to be parents.

The parents who need to step up to their responsibilities are not the ones reading this book.

Those who have stayed the course of parenthood need to insist that our contemporaries do the same.

This country has enough abandoned kids who are still living at home.

They have been abandoned in their own household.

I am the guy who says, "That dog don't hunt."

Government policies won't fix what responsible Americans won't do first.

We are our brother's keeper.

Among the top things that our brothers and sisters need is a charge from the rest of us to *be a parent*.

For that charge to be legitimate, it must come with the concomitant that we will mentor those who are off course.

To simply say "It's time to be a parent" is judgmental. Christians have stern warnings about judging and condemning others. We must speak the truth in love but realize that for things to change for the better, we cannot just sit on the sidelines, saying, "I told you so."

> So just who am I to talk about someone else's kids?
> I am the guy who says let's challenge parents to be parents.
> I am the guy who says let's not take any excuse for not parenting.
> I am the guy who says we must not have mercy and compassion only for the children; we must demonstrate such mercy as mentors to the adults as well.
> Both tasks must be done with love.

Had I picked up someone else's book or article or found my way to somebody's blog espousing these things, I would have asked, "Just who is this character?"

Hopefully, I have given you a reconnaissance of the problem at hand and my first hand experience.

I do believe there are meaningful things that we can do to change our local communities so the term *throwaway kids* becomes obsolete.

Are you up to the challenge?

When the day's work was over, the owner of the vineyard instructed his foreman, "Call the workers in and pay them their wages. Start with the last hired and go on to the first."

Those hired at five o'clock came up and were each given a dollar. When those who were hired first saw that, they assumed they would get far more. But they got the same, each of them one dollar. Taking the dollar, they groused angrily to the manager, "These last workers put in only one easy hour, and you just made them equal to us, who slaved all day under a scorching sun."

He replied to the one speaking for the rest, "Friend, I haven't been unfair. We agreed on the wage of a dollar, didn't we? So take it and go. I decided to give to the one who came last the same as you. Can't I do what I want with my own money? Are you going to get stingy because I am generous?"

Here it is again, the Great Reversal: many of the first ending up last, and the last first.

—Matthew 20:8–16 (The Message)

TOM SPENCE

It's Not Fair

Most parents of *throwaway kids* think that they are the ones unfairly treated. Life owed them something and it hasn't delivered. It is nearly impossible to love another person when you are in a perennial pity party.

> We are not owed anything.
> We are called to love each other.
> We should be our brother's keeper.
> We should treat others as we expect to be treated.

So let's reverse roles.

If we who are reading this book were not the proactive, hardworking, and industrious people that we are today, but somehow were struggling each month just to keep the water from being cut off, up to our neck in bills, and so unhappy with the way our life had turned out that zoning out with beer, booze, or some other substance designed to make the world go away, *would we want someone to show us another way?*

The answer is probably *no*!

No? Really? Why?

Because we just said that we are not proactive, hardworking, or industrious! That's not who we are and we have become comfortable with who we are. There is both comfort and satisfaction in seeing ourselves as victims. We are not responsible for anything. Stuff just happens to us. Somebody else needs to take care of anything important—including our kids.

And we—the readers of this book—collectively say, *"No way!"*

I would want help out of my helplessness.

Really, because we would have to leave our comfort zone and that, by definition, is uncomfortable.

No, really, I would want some help. I would deal with the challenge of stepping out of my comfort zone to do right by my family, especially my children.

Really?

Then why have we not stepped out of our comfort zone as proactive, hard-working, and industrious people to reach out to those who just don't seem to care. Why don't we reach out to those who can't make ends meet? Why don't we help those whose lives are simply a mess?

We do! We feed their kids. We buy them clothes each year. We got them backpacks and supplies for school. We do reach out!

Are we really willing to reach out and help?

We will do anything to help fix this mess!

Why don't we reach out to the parents?

We will do anything, but I won't do that. That's another story. It's hard talking with another adult about changing his or her life.

So let's summarize.

If we were hopelessly addicted to self pity, with few resources at our disposal, and disposed to having no responsibility for our own lives, much less our families; then we would step out of our comfort zone and do something differently?

But if we loathe self pity, have a reasonable amount of resources at our disposal (you had enough to buy this book and the time to read it), and preach responsibility and righteous living; then we would not step out of our comfort zone to do something differently?

We would not speak the truth in love to the parents of the children that we help so often?

Really?

It boils down to courage.

Will we who know a better way lead those who cannot see it.

Will we do it without condemnation?

Will we do it with love?

Will we do it as if we were doing it for our own flesh and blood?

That doesn't seem fair. It seems like those who screwed up ought to have to do something! It's just not fair that those who have done so little take so much effort.

Or, there is another way to look at it.

> For God so loved the world that he gave his one and only Son, that whoever believes in him shall not perish but have eternal life.
>
> —John 3:16 (NIV)

This should sound familiar too.

> You see, at just the right time, when we were still powerless, Christ died for the ungodly. Very rarely will anyone die for a righteous person, though for a good person someone might possibly dare to die. But God demonstrates his own love for us in this: While we were still sinners, Christ died for us.
>
> —Romans 5:6–8 (NIV)

It is really not about fairness at all. It is about grace. God loved us when we were unlovable. He didn't wait for us to take the first step.

Somewhere along the way those of us who seem to negotiate the world well enough that we don't live in fear of being evicted or having our car repossessed or having the water cut off every other month decided that those who are in that predicament should have to dig themselves out of it before we would be willing to help.

Somehow we forgot the grace of God and got comfortable in the judgment seat.

Do these parents of *throwaway kids* need to do something?

Absolutely!

But we go first.

We get to say words that Jesus used.

We get to say words that every infantry leader knows.

We get to say *follow me*!

"Follow me" says that I have made a commitment to get you where you need to go. I am not carrying you. I am not pampering you. I am not condemning you. I am not being condescending. I am leading.

All things considered, my human nature says that I deserve to be at home watching my favorite show on my big screen television with an ice cold beverage at the ready, but I have decided instead to lead.

Today, we need parents who have been successful to lead those who struggle or have given up. Condemning parents who have neglected or abandoned their parenting duties only reinforces their victim mindset. We become coconspirators in this pity party if we are judgmental.

If we want anything to change, we must be leaders not judges. Not all will follow. Welcome to leadership!

> The servant who knows what his master wants and ignores it, or insolently does whatever he pleases, will be thoroughly thrashed. But if he does a poor job through ignorance, he'll get off with a slap on the hand. Great gifts mean great responsibilities; greater gifts, greater responsibilities!
>
> Luke 12:47–48 (The Message)

It sounds like there is no rest for the diligent, for the successful, for those who use their talents wisely.

Sure there is. There is plenty of rest. There is, however, no retiring from leadership.

There was nothing like kicking back for an evening after a twenty-five-mile forced march in full gear. Such gatherings might have involved a couple beers, a few cigars, and those who made the journey. The camaraderie after taking on such a challenge was ten times that of just meeting a few friends for a couple drinks and casual conversation.

Having spent yourself in a good cause and being in the company of those who shared the experience is paradoxically better rest than going home and just soaking sore, blistered feet.

Too often when we say rest, we mean retirement. We want out of the responsibility business. We want out of the leadership business. Let somebody else take it from here.

It sounds like we desire the lifestyle of those whom we need to be helping. Ouch!

We who have the greater gifts must step up to greater responsibility, not withdraw to retirement.

We must not covet complacency.

What good is a navigator if he only gets himself to the destination?

We must become leaders who have no tolerance for the entitlement mentality—to include within ourselves—and blaze a trail for those lost in the wilderness of believing themselves to be a victim. We know the way out. We must lead them.

Start saying these words to yourself for you will soon need to be saying them to others:

Follow me!

Resistance

Follow me!

There's nothing like those words. In fact when you say them to a bunch of Marines, you had better be able to stay in front of them.

But we are not leading Marines. We are leading many people who do not want to go. They don't want to follow. They see neither the goal nor the benefit, only that we are asking them to leave their comfort zone.

Some will actively resist. They won't put out any effort to get out of their mess, but they will exert effort to stay where they are.

Some will be firebrands of discontent.

Some will find a narcotizing effect in discontent and others will graduate to become the bell cows of discontent.

We are given wonderful guidance in Matthew's gospel. *Do not cast your pearls before swine.*

Do not waste your best efforts on the least productive endeavors. Continue to invite, but don't be dragged down into a pig wrestling match. You both will get dirty but the pig will love it.

Some people will only be content in their discontentment.

But some will follow.

Some will begin to take a real interest in what their children are doing at school.

Some will return their folders signed.

Some may eventually add a thank you note to the teacher.

Some may not smoke for two days to save enough to send two children on the field trip to the farm adventure or the movie theater.

Some may bring their children to church.

Some may get out and come into the worship service instead of just the high speed drop off and escape.

Some may come to a Sunday school class to try to learn about being a new creation.

Some will repent and seek forgiveness.

Some will actively seek help in making a budget.

Some will actively seek help in addressing their addictions.

Some will actively seek you to pray with them.

Some may actually make an offering to God.

We who lead must not be discouraged by those who do not follow. That detracts from what we give to those who are following.

We who lead are not permitted self pity.

THROW AWAY KIDS

We who lead detest self pity.

We give self pity no purchase in our lives or our leadership.

We have full permission to confront those who are not content to just stay home but who also must entice their neighbors not to leave the pity party so early.

Marines have a saying.

Lead, follow, or get out of the way.

You are leading. Some are following. Tell the malcontents to get out of the way.

Don't converse, argue, or otherwise become engaged with such firebrands of discontent. Their objective is to drag you down so the narcotizing effects of their self-pity do not wear off.

These people are neither sincere nor worth your time.

Invite.

Lead those who follow.

Tell those who obstruct to get out of the way. That is the extent of the conversation required.

How heartless!

No, how loving.

You would not give an addict booze or crack. Why give one addicted to discontent what he or she is craving.

Maybe the next time someone says, "Follow me," the pity addict will have bottomed out and want to follow.

Don't drag anyone along. They become a burden upon those trying to be freed from their burdens. Lead those who follow and boldly tell the malcontents to get out of the way.

We lead those who are following.

We show them how to make a budget.

We show them what a sound basic daily routine is.

We show them the value of a relationship with God.

We show them the value of a relationship with our families.

We live the value of our relationship with those parents who are following.

Our leadership is transformational, not transactional.

We detested those who came to the church seeking money as if they were using a vending machine. Say the magic words, money comes out.

We don't like being used.

Those we lead don't like being used either.

They are not a means to an end.

It's not, fix the parents and get a better community or nation, though that will surely be a byproduct.

It is to lead the parents to better relationships with their children, their children's teachers, their children's Sunday school teachers, and others with whom and through whom they become a vital part of the community.

The first relationship that must be established as genuine is with us. We must let those who follow know that we are in this for the long haul. It's not just, "I'll get you started then you are on your own."

We must become a guide, a navigator, a change agent, and yes a mentor. True mentors are lifelong guides.

Are we willing to make ourselves available to others for as long as it takes?

To make this commitment is to begin a genuine relationship.

If you are just willing to help these somewhat dysfunctional parents until you think they can help themselves, then you don't have the leadership credentials. You may have the skills but not the commitment.

What is worse than those who don't follow?

A leader who begins and then quits, abandoning those in trace leaves them more disoriented and dysfunctional than before, and surely more distrustful of those beckoning them from their current state.

Many will not follow because they are certain of one thing. The leader is not certain of his or her commitment. Followers fear that leaders will bug out at the first sign of trouble. Part is conjecture. Part is experience. Some is anecdotal from the conjecture and experience of others.

Leaders must build more than rapport. They must build trust. Trust comes from experiencing the genuine commitment of the leader.

For those who truly want to remedy the problem of *throwaway kids*, we must commit to staying the course with the parents.

We are not the Pied Piper of Hamlin leading masses of children, but peer mentors leading two or three adults at any one time. At some point, those who follow will need less frequent challenge and support and the leader may opt to begin anew with others who rejected the first *follow me* invitation. Recent protégés could be brought in to assist in this mentoring process so as to later become mentors as well.

Okay.

I'm in.

I will lead or mentor or navigate two or maybe three parents. I will stick with them and do my part to develop this life-long relationship.

TOM SPENCE

I don't even know who I am going to help and I'm committing to a long-term relationship.

Am I serious or delirious?

You are entering the world of *Koinoni*a.

This is true Christian fellowship. This is true community. This is a community where there are none whom we might describe as *the least of these my brothers.*

All are our brothers and sisters in Christ.

This is not because of a screening process but because of an inclusion process. Those on the fringes are brought into the center. No one is left out. No one feels excluded. All are part of the family of faith. All are part of God's community.

I thought fellowship was a cup of coffee and a doughnut between Sunday school and church?

Fellowship is often associated with food and drink. These are a part of fellowship. The community does eat, but they are not central. It is the community—the inclusion—that constitutes the fellowship.

I thought we were talking about resistance? How did we get to fellowship?

Through leadership, mentoring, navigating, and commitment, that's how we got to *Koinonia*.

We don't fight the resistance. We lead and love those who follow.

We bring those outside into the community.

They don't earn their way in.

We lead them.

We love them.

We become God's love to them.

There is no "in group" and "out group."

There is the community.

We call it the covenant community, the family of faith, and even the body of Christ; but it is the community known by God's love.

Leadership is love.

Love is the strongest force in the universe. It beats logic and reason, intimidation, and even enticement every time.

Love thrives in community.

A Prayer for *Koinonia*

Offer this prayer to God individually or as a group with a common purpose.

> Father in Heaven, we come before your throne:
>
> That we seek service over selfishness.
> That you open our eyes to the trust you have placed in us.
> That we surrender our God-given talents and Spiritual Gifts to produce fruit.
> That you open our hearts so you may fill them with love.
> That we become your love during this special time.
>
> That when we are poured out and have no more, you fill us.
> That when we feel exhausted, you refresh us.
> That when we hold on to personal preferences, you extract them from us.
> That when we see no other options, you ignite the creative spirit in us.
> That when we gravitate to those we know the best, you lead us to those we know the least.

That this mission never be a burden,
In our minds,
To our bodies,
For our spirit,
Or in our heart that we have given to you.

That we find your joy as we serve,
Through our sacrifice,
Through our suffering,
Through our humbleness,
And by being love as you are love.
Amen.

If we bring parents into the community of love, how much more likely to love their children will they be?

If we value our relationship with parents who have answered the call to *follow me*, how much more likely are they to value their relationship with their children, with school faculty, with pastors and elders, with community leaders, and with their neighbors?

Love, not judgment, overcomes resistance.

Love conquers all.

Love calls us to lead, mentor, guide, navigate and commit to all who chose to follow.

Love compels us to speak of One who called to us and said, "Follow me."

Love compels us to speak in the first person of the One we follow.

Love compels us to be the witnesses of Jesus Christ in this world, especially to the parents who have trusted us.

Jesus has overcome the world.

He has told us that we will do greater things than he did.

Being loving leaders and mentors to parents who have dropped off the responsibility grid is one of those greater things.

Very truly I tell you, whoever believes in me will do the works I have been doing, and they will do even greater things than these, because I am going to the Father. And I will do whatever you ask in my name, so that the Father may be glorified in the Son. You may ask me for anything in my name, and I will do it.

—John 14:12–14 (NIV)

Laundry List

I'm not going to judge.

I am going to lead.

I do commit to stay the course.

I will witness with my love and my words.

I will include those who follow in the family of faith.

None will feel as if they are the least of these.

I believe that love never fails.

But what exactly is it that I need to do?

In my experience as a parent, some things just came natural or were easy to figure out. I didn't take notes as I went along. I'm not sure what I need to teach or demonstrate or make recommendations about. I need a checklist.

Then start making one. No two lists need be alike. The list is never in stone. It will change. Trial and error is still a viable mode.

Do this in conjunction with the parents you are helping. This is not the time for an expert and idiot experience. Share not only your expertise, but your trials, your solutions, your failures, your laughs, and your dearest memories. Be real. Make your checklists together.

Remember back to when you were new parents. This can be scary. Why? Because before you were new parents, you were expert parents.

We all knew exactly what to do when we looked at everyone else's kids, but subsequently had this universally shared epiphany when we had our own children. *I don't know everything I thought I did.*

I love that the church that I pastor has so many babies. I think that we are on a streak of about a dozen girls in a row. Our youth group will double in size in about twelve to fourteen years when all the boys start coming here.

It's fun to watch the babies. It is more fun to watch the parents. Those first few times that their baby drops the pacifier on the floor there is a process of rushing it to the sink to prewash it in hot water, then two cycles in the dishwasher or one in boiling water, then the parents sanitize their hands, give the pacifier one last inspection, and carefully put it back in the child's mouth praying that no germs got in. They end up buying six packs of pacifiers. This is a laborious process.

A few weeks later, the child drops the pacifier on the floor; mom catches it on the bounce, wipes it on her shirt, pops it in her own mouth, and then puts it back in her baby's own mouth, thinking, "She will need those germs to help strengthen her immune system."

Back when we were expert parents such a practice was unthinkable.

Once we became real parents we learned to take one day at a time. Our love for our children was and is forever, but so much of our parenting is learned and refined on the run.

Parenting is not an option. We are parents. We don't quit being parents. The only thing we give in to is love. We may not be able to figure out the best sequence to get the kids dressed, and fed, and safely to the bus stop, but we don't stop trying, and we surely don't compromise on love.

> Never give in—never, never, never, never, in nothing great or small, large or petty, never give in except to convictions of honour and good sense. Never yield to force; never yield to the apparently overwhelming might of the enemy.
>
> —Winston Churchill

Write a plan. Plan getting ready for school. Plan cooking healthy meals. Plan a time for family prayer and Bible reading. Plan time for showers and bathing. Plan time for homework. Plan kid-free time (yes, when you start parenting for real you must plan some time just for husband and wife).

Putting something in writing triggers more thinking in the mind. Note the obstacles.

- Sleepy headed kids.
- Sleepy headed mom or dad.
- Finicky eaters.
- Rooms in disarray.
- School times and work times in conflict.

Get creative with solutions.

Come on, people!

This is life! We are made in the image of a creative God. Be creative!

Find creative ways to overcome obstacles.

Find creative ways to redo the entire plan.

And then—then—don't get married to your plan.

What! All that planning and you tell me not to put it into concrete?

Exactly! Don't take all of the life out of life with a rigid plan.

Your love for your children is inviolate.

The daily routine needs some flexibility. Let your children be involved.

Increase self awareness. We are the most self aware creatures on the planet. We can mentally step outside of ourselves and examine what we thought and what we did and ask, "Why did I do that? What would I do differently next time?"

We are self aware. We know that we exist. We know that we think. Unlike the cattle that graze near my home, we have more conscious choices. Poor cattle, they only have two career choices: *Milk or Meat?*

The more we are aware of ourselves, our thoughts, our actions, and our surroundings, the more options we see in negotiating problems. The more visible the alternatives become for exploring opportunities.

But you have to be alive to live.

That really makes sense?

Let's try it this way. Drifting through life in a semiconscious state is not living. Being a party to the smiles, giggles, tears, and apprehensions of you children is living.

Remember the old saying, "You've got to stop and smell the roses?" Add to that the newly mown hay or the freshly cut yard. Add to that the smell of the air after a heavy rain. Add to that the majesty of a sunset or the endless possibilities of a sun rise. Add to that the self-portrait that your son brought home this afternoon from school.

Don't trade these events and moments in for *gotta do's*.
I've got to get the kids to school.
I've got to make something for supper.
I've got to clean the bathroom.
I've got to buy more toilet paper.
I've got to get more sleep.
I've got to be home before the bus gets there.

Gotta, gotta, gotta!
Really?

> Whatever you do, work at it with all your heart, as working for the Lord, not for human masters, since you know that you will receive an inheritance from the Lord as a reward. It is the Lord Christ you are serving.
>
> —Colossians 3:23–24 (NIV)

Maybe it's not *gotta*, but *get to*.

All of those things that we feel we must do as part of some universal labor law could instead be labors of love.

For a decade, I have typed my wife's school newsletter. She develops the content. I simply apply the keystrokes. I, of course, overplay what an onerous task this is that has been placed upon me, always at the worst possible moment, and how it may in some way cause the universe to unravel. I am rather certain that upon my passing, the coroner will discover some latent thespian tendencies as my most likely cause of death.

That said, I wouldn't miss doing this newsletter for the world. It's basically the same year after year, but each year I see if I can't add something to make the spacing or bulletizing or syntax more appealing. This could be a *gotta do* but it's always a *get to do*.

I am fully aware that how I approach the task—my ability to act upon my environment—is life changing. I wouldn't let anyone else do that newsletter for love nor money.

As we move to being responsible parents, our list needs to have mostly *get to do's* and not so many *gotta do's*.

Be practical. First grade children are not going to do four hours of homework every night. Children up to first grade should be read to every night. After that, ask them to read to you.

Be methodical. Don't over script, but get in a grove for the important stuff: Prayer time, homework time, having a meal together time.

Be healthy. Clean teeth, clean clothes, and clean bodies are not options. Something in the area of fast food, alcohol, tobacco, movie rentals, or owning the newest video game might need to go to the back burner so the water doesn't get cut off. Some more nice to have items might have to wait for another day so that you have gas or electricity to heat water for showers and baths.

This is not an extremely sacrificial lifestyle. It is living within your means.

Health also entails what goes into the mind and body. It costs about the same to eat a healthy home cooked meal as it does to eat junk. It may take a while to wean your family off junk. This does not have to be a now and forever more moment when the roast, rice, and carrots replace sliders and pizza rolls, but the latter should become the exception for both health and financial reasons.

Perhaps one of the toughest intakes to measure and monitor is what comes into both the adult and juvenile minds via television, internet, and video games.

You have heard of GIGO: Garbage In, Garbage Out. But it's worse than that. The garbage never really is expunged. That's right, what we hear and see registers in both our short- and long-term memories. We can purge some of this, but only if the input stops or is slowed down significantly.

The apostle Paul wrote to a church in Rome almost two thousand years ago telling them that to change the way they lived into something acceptable to God, they had to change their minds.

Literally, they needed to replace the mind that they had which had conformed to the patterns of their time and start over with a new one.

The good news is that this did not and does not require brain surgery.

It does require a scalpel.

You need to circumscribe your life, especially your thought life. Nothing gets in but what should get in.

Think of circling the wagons around your mind. Think of the Marines defending a hilltop and being attacked from all sides. No one gets through the perimeter.

Cut a circle around your mind—around your life. No junk gets into our thinking.

We have choices.

- The television has an "off" setting (this may be news to some). Use it.

- Video games are not a right. Regulate their usage. Know what's in the game.

- The next generation cell phone has a new feature: human mode. You can leave the phone off and out of sight and talk to people face to face.

- Be the master of all of the technology in your home.

- You decide what is healthy.

Be focused. You made a grocery list. Stick to it. Don't fall for the store ploys that weave you in an endless serpentine course so that you must walk by everything to get to the eight items you came for. Make a list. Stick to it. Don't succumb to losing your focus, spending your paycheck, and wondering, "How did I end up broke with this load of junk."

Be Love! Paul wrote to the church that he had established in Corinth, Greece. They were a new church in a faith that was just understanding what it meant to live by the Spirit, and they had some things to sort out. One of them was the gifts that God had bestowed upon believers and another was how these believers were treating each other. Both needed some course corrections. Translators have marked thirteen verses in the thirteenth chapter of Paul's first letter to this church.

1 Corinthians 13 (NIV)

If I speak in the tongues of men or of angels, but do not have love, I am only a resounding gong or a clanging cymbal. If I have the gift of prophecy and can fathom all mysteries and all knowledge, and if I have a faith that can move mountains, but do not have love, I am nothing. If I give all I possess to the poor and give over my body to hardship that I may boast, but do not have love, I gain nothing.

Love is patient, love is kind. It does not envy, it does not boast, it is not proud. It does not dishonor others, it is not self-seeking, it is not easily angered, it keeps no record of wrongs. Love does not delight in evil but rejoices with the truth. It always protects, always trusts, always hopes, always perseveres.

Love never fails. But where there are prophecies, they will cease; where there are tongues, they will be stilled; where there is knowledge, it will pass away. For we know in part and we prophesy in part, but when completeness comes, what is in part disappears.

TOM SPENCE

When I was a child, I talked like a child, I thought like a child, I reasoned like a child. When I became a man, I put the ways of childhood behind me. For now we see only a reflection as in a mirror, then we shall see face to face. Now I know in part; then I shall know fully, even as I am fully known.

And now these three remain: faith, hope and love. But the greatest of these is love.

We can make the best checklist in the world, but if it is not laced with love—genuine love—it's a waste of time and paper. The worst checklist in the world saturated with love will enable a parent to find a way to be a parent. Love won't let self-pity spend the night. Love won't give up on reading to a son or daughter. Love will change that diaper for the sixteenth time today. Love will stop and listen to what happened at school today and be excited to see what her precious child did in class today. Love will make two packets of Ramen and a can of corn into a feast and will set the table for a banquet. Love will offer thanks where the human heart sees nothing for which to be thankful.

Love never fails.

What does that mean with regard to our laundry list?

It is not so much that you accounted for everything that might happen in a day or a week or between paychecks; but that you accounted for love in every day or week or challenge between paychecks.

But as this chapter purports a list of some sort, here it is.

1. Parenting is not an option
2. Write a plan

3. Increase self awareness
4. Be practical
5. Be methodical
6. Be healthy
7. Be focused
8. Be Love!

> Jesus looked at them and said, "With man this is impossible, but with God all things are possible."
>
> Matthew 19:26 (NIV)

Repetition

Does practice make perfect?

Anyone who has ever taught or been a student in the cognitive restructuring class, *Thinking for a Change*, knows the answer.

Does practice make perfect?

No! Perfect practice makes perfect.

If you don't believe it, take up the game of golf. If your swing is a mess but you do one hundred repetitions of this swing with each club in your bag, your swing will still be a mess. You must practice a new or revised swing to get different results.

Other than the moment of conception, parenting requires repetition.

Setting good habits early makes parenting easier.

Establishing good habits to replace old, less desirable ones takes repetition.

It takes repetition of the new desirable habits. This is perhaps one of the greatest challenges for parents who have given up or only do what they must to avoid being pursued by the law for child neglect. This is work—real work.

It requires commitment from the parents.

It is not a reasonable goal for most parents with *throwaway kids*. They just can't do it.

That's not quite true.

They just can't do it alone.

We must be encouragers and the parents must trust in the One who can do all things.

Changing old habits is the *getting a camel through the eye of the needle* for modern-day parents who have given up. It is not possible without God.

God intends to use us as encouragers.

The parent struggling in this journey will be tempted to quit.

We will be tempted to judge.

Both parties must petition God for not only the strength, will power, and stick-to-itiveness needed; but also for the peace of God that goes beyond understanding while we pursue the impossible. Both guide and follower are scaling Mount Everest and are afraid of falling. God's peace is not an optional piece of gear. It is the *sine qua non*. A parent going through daily hell—living without God's peace—is not likely to finish the parenting journey for which you are the guide.

> Do not be anxious about anything, but in every situation, by prayer and petition, with thanksgiving, present your

requests to God. And the peace of God, which transcends all understanding, will guard your hearts and your minds in Christ Jesus.

Philippians 4:6–7

Both mentor and protégé must petition God with thanksgiving and live in a peace that does not make sense compared to the magnitude of the task ahead.

With God and God's peace, parents will acquire new habits, better habits, and eventually catch the idiom—the rhythm—of parenting.

This is too important a calling to ever give up on.

Sometimes we just get ourselves and the ones we are leading through this day.

One more repetition of good parenting.

One more rep.

Just one more.

A Calling

I have some experience with being called.

Some folks may enter ordained ministry because they think they are a good people person. *Ouch! They are in for a surprise.*

Some folks may enter ordained ministry because they have studied the Bible a lot. *Good luck.*

Some people may enter ordained ministry because they have good public speaking skills. *May the force be with you.*

Why the dryness with regard to this topic?

Because without a genuine calling, most of those who entered the ministry will be both frustrated and miserable. Some will quit. Some will continue in their ministry of misery. Some will eventually find some peace in their vocation. Some will simply conform to the world and just treat ministry as a job.

There is nothing wrong with good people skills, a solid biblical background, and even the ability to turn a phrase from a lectern or pulpit; however, the *sine qua non* of the call to ordained ministry is the call to ordained ministry.

God calls and the recipient will have no peace until he or she answers. Many have resisted, ran away, or just continued in a multiyear or multidecade denial, but God continues his calling.

I resisted.
I rationalized.
I was sure that I was unsure that the voice speaking to me was God.
I was wrong. It was him.
Resistance is futile.

Answering the call gave me peace.
I still had much to learn.
I still had much to experience.
There was still hard work ahead of me.

But once I answered the call, the magnitude of the task was no longer overwhelming. I was moving forward. Some steps were bigger than others, but the thought of not continuing on my prescribed course no longer existed.

I was not entitled to that thought.
How restrictive!

No! How liberating! I am ordained by God to be a minister of Word and Sacrament. That is my identity. I am free to engage my entire being in this calling.

And it is not so different for parents.
Some of us got that right off.

Somewhere in the twinkling of an eye, conception, delivery, and first smelly diaper change sequence—some of us *got it* that we were parents.

There was no going back.
The time for second thoughts had passed.

That was our identity. It wasn't a temporary duty assignment. We were parents for life. We are parents for life. Even when your kids are grown and have kids of their own, you are still a parent.

Sometimes they come back and move in with you just to remind you, but even if they live on the other side of the planet, you are still their parents.

Some who have no children of their own, and perhaps cannot have their own kids, are also called to be parents. Thanks be to God for them! They have rescued many a child from being a ward of the state. They have rescued a child from a life without a real parent. They have rescued children from a life without much love or hope.

And some who have conceived children have never answered the call to be parents. Some have run from the call. Some just don't think it's fair that they are responsible for another life, or two, or three.

Some deny the call.

But the calling to be a parent is as real and as tangible as the one to ordained ministry. It is also more ubiquitous.

Few are called to the clergy.

The vast majority of adults are called to parenting.

The challenge for reluctant parent and willing mentor is to recognize the calling. It is not an option. Life doesn't get better the longer you resist the call.

The good news for the mentor is that those who are currently following your lead at least suspect this to be the truth. Those who don't are not in your entourage anyway.

So what are we to do?

How do we help reinforce this?

Use the title "parent" or "parents" in casual conversation, formal address, and as a little status recognition.

"We parents need to look out for each other."

"Parents, don't forget to say thank you to your child's teacher this week."

"We have something special for the parents today."

"It's good to be a parent."

Help the parents write a mission statement, or at least a mantra of some sorts.

> We the parents of Joanne and Robert, in order to provide a loving home, establish a place of safety, provide for the basic needs of our wonderful children, promote the gospel of love…

Have some fun with this, but insist upon the element of parental identity in these exercises.

The parental identity is both individual and corporate. Sharing experiences reinforces the calling.

> Parenting isn't just biological.
> It isn't just psychological.
> Sometimes it isn't even logical.
> But it is our identity.

Once we accept this, once our protégés accept this, we are no longer scaling Mt. Everest. We are just hiking up Mt. Fuji. It's still a challenge, but over half a million regular people walk to the top each year.

> Why are we parents?
> Because that's who we are.
> That's fuzzy math, or at least circular logic.
> No, that's identity.

We who lead are not leading into the wilderness. We are leading out of the wilderness to a homeland.

It's a homeland for parents.
It is where parents are called to be.
Our loving leadership is to bring the parents home.

Closing without Conclusion

We who are Christians will take care of the children. We will not let them be discarded. My hope is that the term *throwaway kids* was distasteful to all who read this. My hope is that you were called to action.

My prayer is for courage.
Some must lead.
Some must step forward.
Some must answer the call to be leaders and mentors.
We are made to serve each other.

Feeding kids, filling backpacks with school supplies, and delivering a message of love with genuineness in speech and deed is the easy part.

Leading parents out of dysfunction takes gumption.

If you get almost to the end of the Bible, there is a passage about those you would expect to get their comeuppance.

Who?

The unbelieving, the vile, the murderers, the sexually immoral, those who practice magic arts, the idolaters, and all liars—folks that most people probably would not be surprised to find there.

But that is not the entire verse. Consider Revelation 21:8 in its entirety.

> But the cowardly, the unbelieving, the vile, the murderers, the sexually immoral, those who practice magic arts, the idolaters and all liars—they will be consigned to the fiery lake of burning sulfur. This is the second death.

What?

The cowardly are lumped in with murderers and idolaters?

God desires none to perish, but apparently you are running in the same crowd with someone who took a life with malice aforethought and those who worship Baal or a big rock statue or maybe even a rock star when you live a life of cowardice.

The Old Testament lists several things which God finds detestable or an abomination. We can get our minds around some of those.

But cowardice?

That seems more like just a human frailty than something as ugly as murder.

It gives us pause to think and meditate and perhaps consider a little more direction from God's word.

The Parable of the Talents

> Again, it will be like a man going on a journey, who called his servants and entrusted his property to them. To one he gave five talents of money, to another two talents, and to another one talent, each according to his ability. Then he went on his journey. The man who had received the five talents went at once and put his money to work and gained five more. So also, the one with the two talents gained two

more. But the man who had received the one talent went off, dug a hole in the ground and hid his master's money.

After a long time the master of those servants returned and settled accounts with them. The man who had received the five talents brought the other five. "Master," he said, "you entrusted me with five talents. See, I have gained five more."

His master replied, "Well done, good and faithful servant! You have been faithful with a few things; I will put you in charge of many things. Come and share your master's happiness!"

The man with the two talents also came. "Master," he said, "you entrusted me with two talents; see, I have gained two more."

His master replied, "Well done, good and faithful servant! You have been faithful with a few things; I will put you in charge of many things. Come and share your master's happiness!"

Then the man who had received the one talent came. "Master," he said, "I knew that you are a hard man, harvesting where you have not sown and gathering where you have not scattered seed. So I was afraid and went out and hid your talent in the ground. See, here is what belongs to you."

His master replied, "You wicked, lazy servant! So you knew that I harvest where I have not sown and gather where I have not scattered seed? Well then, you should have put my money on deposit with the bankers, so that when I returned I would have received it back with interest.

"Take the talent from him and give it to the one who has the ten talents. For everyone who has will be given more, and he will have an abundance. Whoever does not have, even what he has will be taken from him. And throw that worthless servant outside, into the darkness, where there will be weeping and gnashing of teeth."

—Matthew 25:14–30 (NIV)

We all must ask ourselves a question. It's the same question for all of us. It's one that we expect God to ask us one day.

What did you do with what I gave you?

Did we use the gifts, talents, opportunities, resources, and blessings of our lives to produce a good return for our Master?

All of the servants in this parable surely experienced some encounter with fear. The first two had likely addressed it previously. The master already trusted them more than the third.

The third servant was immobilized by fear to some extent. He was still able to compose his excuses, but could not compose a first step to doing something with what he had been given.

Our Master understands that we have fear. In fact, he told us that to fear God was the beginning point in a good relationship. Knowledge and wisdom would follow from such a foundation.

He also is not pleased when we make that fear bigger than the gifts that he gave us. To not use our gifts is not to trust God.

To not use our gifts in helping others is to believe that what God has called us to do is less satisfying that what we would have done with that time and effort.

To not use our talents and resources to help others is to deny our destiny. We receive blessings for the purpose of blessing others.

To not use our opportunities to help others is to believe that whatever we do instead will bring greater satisfaction than our

Master telling us: "Well done, good and faithful servant! You have been faithful with a few things; I will put you in charge of many things. Come and share your master's happiness!"

To not help others is to not trust God.
It is not wise.
It is not recommended.
It is cowardly.

I don't believe that God wants us to do things because we are afraid of the consequences. It's hard to produce a good return on investment when your actions are motivated by fear.

I do believe that we should understand clearly what pleases God.
Blessing others—yes!
Cowardice—no!

Speaking the truth in love takes courage.
God will empower you with his strength.
His own Spirit was sent to walk beside you.
You are not in this alone.

We are called to be a living sacrifice.
That is our very lives are set apart to be used for God's purpose.
The time, money, effort, and things that we give up to lead other adults with children into the promised land of parenthood are our reasonable act of worship.

They are part of our sacrifice.
They are holy and pleasing to God.
They are absolutely worth it!

TOM SPENCE

Don't fool yourself into thinking that you are a listener when you are anything but, letting the Word go in one ear and out the other. Act on what you hear! Those who hear and don't act are like those who glance in the mirror, walk away, and two minutes later have no idea who they are, what they look like.

But whoever catches a glimpse of the revealed counsel of God—the free life!—even out of the corner of his eye, and sticks with it, is no distracted scatterbrain but a man or woman of action. That person will find delight and affirmation in the action.

—James 1:22–25 (The Message)

Implementation

The word of the day, of the week, of the year and decade is *fonly*.

Don't look it up in the dictionary. The definition there will say "foolish or fondly," but that's not what it means.

Fonly is how we say "if only." People say it so much that it blends into a single word.

Fonly.

How should we define this contraction of *if only*?

- The death of initiative
- A perennial excuse for inaction
- A procrastinator's self-pardoning phrase
- Cowardice by any other name
- Having a tight grip on hopelessness
- An excuse addict's score
- The kingpin of inaction
- Addicted to one's current state
- Fear

The list could go on. Add two or three of your own. It should be easy because you have seen these two words—*if only*—kill recovery from drug addiction, marriage reconciliation, qualification for scholarships or competitive jobs, and so much more.

TOM SPENCE

What are the antonyms of *Fonly*?

- Action
- First steps
- Just Do It
- Courage

How do we implement something that is needed nationwide? One person at a time.

Begin by mentoring one person who needs help being a parent. You may have to invite half a dozen, but when you find one, just get to work.

Don't wait for the government, the local church, the neighborhood community center, or a sequel to this book to begin.

Just do it.

I make no apologies to the shoe company that took my catch phrase and made it into their trademark. How could I?

They just did it! Good on 'em.

And so too the implementation plan for this huge endeavor to bring parents back to parenting begins with your first step to assist one or two other people in need.

The plan is neither coordinated nor synchronized beyond the individual or family level.

God doesn't need ten thousand signatures on a petition to begin blessing your ministry.

He is just waiting on your first steps.

Just do it.

My eyes will be on the faithful in the land,
> that they may dwell with me;
> the one whose walk is blameless
> > will minister to me.

—Psalm 101:6 (NIV)

TOM SPENCE

Some Restrictions Apply

There's always a catch!

Or not.

Dive in head first, but make sure there is water in the pool.

Do not abandon common sense. Do not neglect your sixth sense.

What?

A Christian author spouting out something about a sixth sense?

Try it this way. Bring your intuition and judgment.

Single parent families have different challenges than traditional families.

Same gender mentoring arrangements are best.

If you feel in danger, you just might be. There are evil people in the world. Some of them are just waiting to be invited into your life.

Sometimes you may need to meet in a church or public place where you can have some privacy but also be in the general vicinity of other people.

While mentoring may require interaction at odd hours, home visits should not. If you must make a home visit at odd hours, ask your pastor to accompany you.

This may change as the mentoring relationship grows, but basic safety precautions early in the relationship are essential. Remember that those whom you are helping may also have some apprehension.

Don't abandon your integrity.

If someone says "I'm thinking about killing the next door neighbor" in the course of buying school supplies, you must report them. The folks you are mentoring need to know that you are not a priest and their confessions to you are not in absolute confidence.

If they tell you they have irritable bowel syndrome, you don't need to share that with your friends. If they can't afford toothpaste for the kids but purchase fertilizer by the truckload and have photos of federal buildings in the kitchen, you can share that with as many of your law enforcement contacts as you can.

What am I saying?
There is real danger in the world.
Sometimes dangerous people have children.

Is this a reason to abandon ship?
No.

It is reason to take precautions appropriate to the situation.
Such as?

- Letting a family member or pastor know where you will be in the performance of this ministry.
- Sticking to meeting schedules and places.
- Pursuing this ministry as a married couple's ministry.
- Use the structure available in your area (Volunteer as a mentor at the community action center, your church, or some other organization with some liability protection).

Life has risk.
Love has risk.
Service has risk.
Cowardice has risk.

Don't throw in the towel, abandon ship, sit on your hands, join the *fonly* club, or other figurative way to say give up.

Realize that you are doing real ministry in the real world and you need to consider the risk involved.

That said, I'll abuse Will Rogers just a bit and say that *I never met a risk I couldn't mitigate.*

Few people know the satisfaction of making a real difference in a single life or in a family other than their own.

Few know the joy of sacrifice.

Few truly ask to be God's instrument.

Many complain that something needs to be done.

Few volunteer to be that something or someone.

Mentoring parents of *throwaway kids* is today's call to be *God's Love in Action*.

As you set upon a course to ask God to use you to do his mighty work in a single family, offer the Prayer of St. Francis of Assisi provided on the next page.

You will be blessed.

Prayer of Saint Francis of Assisi

Lord, make me an instrument of your peace.
Where there is hatred, let me sow love;
where there is injury, pardon;
where there is doubt, faith;
where there is despair, hope;
where there is darkness, light;
and where there is sadness, joy.

O Divine Master, grant that I may not so much seek
to be consoled as to console;
to be understood as to understand;
to be loved as to love.
For it is in giving that we receive;
it is in pardoning that we are pardoned;
and it is in dying that we are born to eternal life.
Amen

ABOUT THE AUTHOR

Tom Spence is a retired Marine Corps officer. He is an ordained minister in the Cumberland Presbyterian Church and is the pastor of the church in Burns Flat, Oklahoma.

He is a husband, father, and grandfather, and returned to live in his native Oklahoma in 1999.

Tom publishes hundreds of articles online each year as a freelance author, including two blogs and the local paper.

OTHER TITLES BY TOM SPENCE

Nonfiction

- *God Loves You*
- *Heaven and Hell: Why some people can't get off the subject and on with living*
- *Technology Acquisition & Front End Analysis for the Small Church*
- *ReBaselining America: Setting a foundation of liberty for the next 200 years*
- *Christianity for Marines*
- *Sea Stories*

Fiction

- *Even the Elect*
- *First Steps towards Eternity*
- *Tough Day at the Plate*

Wit and Wisdom Workouts

- *The Best of Out of the Box*

Drama

- *9 Encounters of John 9: A Play in 3 Acts*
- *Ten Talents: A Play in 3 Acts*

Life Skills Education

- *The Profanity Problem: And what to do about it*
- *Acceptance of Authority: Returning to the boundaries of law and ethics*